Poetry, Writings, & Ramblings

By: B.T. Irving

Copyright ©2017 Brandon Irving

Published by: Urban Exchange Publishing

Urbanexchangepub@gmail.com

ISBN13:978-1542533799

ISBN10:1542533791

Dedication

I would like to take this time to dedicate this collection of poetry to three specific friends. First and Foremost, my dear friend Adversity, also known as "the struggle", you have always been there by my side, all my life, although at times I wish it wasn't so. I wouldn't get rid of you even if I had the choice to do so because I have learned some time ago that perseverance builds character and that a person shouldn't wish for things to get easier or less difficult but rather should wish to be better and acquire more skills. You may be ugly on the outside but you certainly have an unparalleled inner beauty.

While we are on the topic of beauty, I might as well bring up my second friend Karma. They say that you reap what you sow and what goes around comes around, they also say that you are a bitch. All these may be true but just like anything else in life, it's all about perspective. Sometimes I'm on your good side and other times not so much. Either way I love you and appreciate all you have done and continue to do in my life.

Third and final but certainly not last, Inspiration. It's as if you come from God himself, I find you in the strangest and most obscure places at the oddest times. You start in my heart and align yourself with my mind and drive me mad until I spill you onto paper, canvas, or dimly lit computer screen. You are the paddle to my boat as I gently roll down this stream of dreams called life. Thankyou friends, this is for you.

Thank You

There are many that I would like to thank, some of you I will not mention on purpose to simply see how you react. I want to first thank Urban Exchange Publishing for publishing my first book and the lovely and talented poet and fellow author and poet K "Quiet" Moore for guiding me in the right direction.

I thank my family and friends for always believing in me, just as I thank the haters and doubters for projecting their insecurities on me and telling me that I'm wasting my time or that I won't ever succeed.

Thank you, mom for birthing your bastard.

Thankyou Joshua Irving for being not only my brother but my keeper.

Thankyou Mary McCrone for being a great friend and mentor and always an inspiration.

Last but not least, thank you Catherine Davis for all you have done the beautiful and terrible a like, a lot of my material has been inspired by what we have put one another through, it has certainly given me perspective.

I AM…

I am so much more than what I let on

I am so much more than you could possibly perceive

I am so much more than what you categorize me

I am a son, a brother, a cousin, a nephew, and a husband

Soon to be ex…

I am a writer, a lover, a fighter, a source of morale, a letdown and an epic fail

I am a bastard, a motherfucker, a douche, and a prick

I am a hero to a few and a villain to many

I am a man

I am a selfish child

I am what goes bump in the night and what creeps in the wild

I am a starving artist, a glutton, a thief, an adulterer

I am a submariner, a sailor, a student, a teacher, a self-righteous preacher

I am loved, I am despised, I am misunderstood, I am full of truth and lies

I am never there when she needs me

I am always there when she needs her space

I am kicked around, bit, stabbed, and punched in the face

I am a survivor, and a victim of circumstance

I am a hopeless romantic without a clue

I am a manipulator and a goon

I am an emaciated mutt howling at the moon

I am an actor who is stuck in character

I am a psychopath and a wretch

I am a visceral youth, handsome and uncouth

I am a hypocrite

I am a brave poltroon

I am still an emaciated mutt howling at the moon

I am a mirage

I am an eclectic collage of all I have endured and encountered

I am still in the making

I am slowly breaking

I am "the devil, a heart breaker, a faggot, a lame, a shell of a man, a loser, a dead beat"

I am a friend, an enemy, a liar, a cheat

I am a care taker, a deal breaker, I am the one who let you out of the cold

I am the one who put those clothes on your back

I am the one who put food in your stomach

I am the one who put a roof over your head

I am the one who broke your heart so many times he's surprised you're not dead

I am the one who holds everything over your head

I am fed up with being struck and stepped on

I am the one who has damn near taken your life but only after countless times of being attacked with a knife

I am the one who fought by your side through demon
oppression and possession

I am insidious and superficial

I am a hard worker and an ingrate

I might just be an infernal reprobate

I am a lover and a fighter

Artist and writer

Your right hand man when you got nothing left

A hedonist and a hell of a chef

I'm a bastard but I ain't no bitch

An asshole but you can't push me down and certainly not
in

I am what I am

I am what I will be and have always been

I am an art exhibit seen by ignorant alien eyes

I am constructively critiqued, discriminated against and
criticized

I am loved, hated, loathed, and despised

Told I am appreciated and I believe such lies

I'm an emo fuck at times

I am a colloquial chameleon

I am humble in my narcissistic arrogant ignorance

I am not coming down from my high horse

This chip on my shoulder throws me off balance

I am a jack of all trades a king of none with various talents

I am loyal but I bite

But never the hand that feeds, unless that hand becomes a
fist and attempts to beat me...

But there are no hands feeding me any longer

I am the hand that feeds

I am the scavenging mutt gradually getting stronger

That will glut the maw of death until it be satiated with the
blood of those who cross me

I am no pure bred, I am cross

I am a drunkard and a glutton for punishment

I am a work horse aspiring to be his own boss

I am a figment of my own imagination

I am a broken and then put back together again with super glue creation

I am a child, jumping and splashing in the rain

Finally, finally outside of the window pane

I am…

I sought to drink her in, her freckle kissed coffee cream
skin glowing in the moonlight

Filled me to the brim with anxious delight

My toes squirming in my shoes

My heart pitter pattering amidst it's indigo hue of still
healing bruised blues

Maybe I was just thirsty and confused

But Oh! How her sable tress did rest on her golden
shoulders and abounded high into the brightly lit night sky
like many cumulous curls

Billowing thunder cloud puffs and tufts accented with
amber as if

Her thoughts could be serenely seen in the gleaming of her
hair; playing with the wind, reaching out and upward in
praise

Her legs went on for days

And she didn't walk but rather glide

Then a little doubt spoke through a pout inside, briefly
subsiding the butterflies

"You don't stand a chance"

But Oh, if I could just get a pacing glance from her angelic
eyes

If I could but be grazed by her grace

Thoughts flooded my mind of her sweet ambrosia waist

I shook them off with a flustered scoff

"Keep it clean"

But, damn she was mean!

In the nicest elegant way that a queen could be

Her disposition alone was a melody

Pearly whites peaked through rose petal lips, pursed in
thought

No, in recognition

I was caught

She observed me appreciating her from a far

She spoke, but I did not hear

Then pain and blackness ever so sudden did rush in

"Look out for that car"

I beg your pardon

Tell me your tale?

The series of unfortunate events that caused your heart to be hardened and your spirit to go stagnant and stale

Why your once fervent hopes and dreams

Turned to ash, blowing away with the wind that was taken from your sails

Did you die because you were forced to make a living?

Absence makes the heart grow fonder

It may also cause your other half to wander

Just as heart break can make your heart stronger

But you must be diligent in these matters

Don't haphazardly handle the shards that have scattered

Take caution

Take time

Take captive

Every thought that enters your mind

Don't give up

Don't give in

Don't settle for less

You will be fine

I promise

We met in a dream

You were convinced it was life

Until you awoke, trembling in a cold sweat

Struggling to remember what you will soon forget

I am not a Human and I'm not a Martian

I'm a demon and angel's botched abortion

Plan-B couldn't stop me

This is the coat hanger banger portion

My Yin and Yang is bang-ah-rang

Peter Pan distortion

There is a hell of a difference

Between a grown kid and a grown man

I have the heart of a child and the soul of an old man

Been through hell and back

Like I was visiting Fam

Like I own a time share there. Damn

I invest in my people and I'm all about my business

They love my goodness

My Guinness

My dark roast flow and they know

I would give the clothes of my back

Just like that

But you're not taking anything from me

Fact!

I will never do a bid

But rest assured, I will break this shiv off under your ribs

Vicious ice age rage like my name is Sid

Off the top like a lid

Smash you before you know what I even did

You're a punk ass kid in a grown man's body

No kiddin'

You struggle to fit in

I get in

I get it in

Yet I stand out and groove

Your personality is back against the wall

Mine is don't just stand there bust a move

The Arsonist's Daughter

She was Satan dressed in satin

Her body language was Latin

I was at a loss for words

Longing to sign language every accentuated curve

But even the deaf have heard

What the blind have observed

And the mute will concur

Play with fire and you get burned

I've been trying to walk right

Despite the constant night

The lamp light only shines on the street so bright

So, my path of enlightenment

Goes to and from with the flow of sporadic traffic

And the wind is always blowing my way

Weathering my reign on a hold of another day

A man can only bend so far until he breaks

And I'm not elastic

I may be a nice guy but I have my spastic tactics

But there is a method to my madness

I can't give specifics

And if I tried to explain my brain it would sound like

Explaining physics to someone who doesn't even speak
English

I have plenty of heart and abound in soul

My plate, my cup, my stomach is full

Sometimes I walk

Others I just roll

Never in a hurry

Stuck on stroll

Look at all these haters like

LOL

Don't tug on what you can't pull and don't try to grasp
what you can't hold

Because it will slip from your grip

And leave your eyes swole

I'm not coming home tonight

And never again

I have fallen from grace one too many times

This time, I was embraced by my sins.

It enveloped me like cold satin sheets

It bound my wrists

It kissed every sore spot I have

It made nothing better

I was going to leave a letter

Only my fetters and chains rang so sweat

Beckoning me to my reckoning

The echo of her voice resounded in my heart and mind

The pain was searing

It deafened my hearing

And caused me to go blind

I went to scream but it was only a crackling gasp of a sigh

I thought, this is it

Then there was a whispered reply

"Never again will you have to cry"

"Just succumb"

"Just submit"

"Surely the numb is better than all pain and this façade of meaningless shit"

I really couldn't argue with it

I had no strength to struggle and no desire to do so

But something just would not let go, and although the pain began to bellow

There was hope

Yet again I lied to my self

As I cried myself to sleep clutching this rope

Flowers don't grow on a submariner's grave

We reside where the devil wouldn't dare

Beneath the cold, cruel blue

Where weeks feel like years

Loved ones seem to be make believe

And screams and cries would fall on deaf ears

Where waves crash violently to no prevail

We're swallowed too deep to care

So, her intimidation fails

All we have is hope to see

The light of day

Praying that all we missed isn't gone to stay

All we have is one another

Like it or not the person you hate is forced to be a brother

Our lives are in one another's hands

This is no job for a coward

So, you must be brave

Flowers don't grow on a submariner's grave

Maybe

Maybe I needed to fall apart

To have everything fall into place

Maybe I needed to learn to appreciate my beauty

By falling on my face

Maybe I should have thrown you out into the cold

Maybe you wouldn't have taken all the warmth

From my heart and soul

My heart is a lyre

My heart is lyre

But you may not pluck its strings

They are reserved

For the girl in the choir

Who so elegantly and angelically sings

Every word abounding in raw emotion

I'm whisked away in her velvety waves

She is a mellifluous ocean

A sweet siren

Calling this sailor to his watery grave

Sleep is the cousin of Death

Whiskey still heavy on my breath

Light hearted burden

Buried deep beneath my Sundays best

On the brink of confessing my sin

To the bastard pastor

I did jest

"If I courted death and the sex was so good that we both
did rest"

"Would it be a threesome a tad bit incestuous?"

The color black

My favorite color is black

You may say

That is the absence of color

And that would actually be a fact

But hey! Look at me not focusing on the lack.

It's perfect on a pair of slick slacks and it matches everything

The abysmal dark ever so wild and stark like the vast night sky

Or the dilated pupil of your lover's eye

Black like ink

Black like coal

Black like ice

Black like my soul

Black like my nieces I love to humbly hold

Black like my tea

Black like the cat that has crossed my path time and time again

Black like me

Black starts with B

Don't mean to be so rudimentary

Black like

Obsidian glow

Ebony gold

Gasoline rainbow

Black is beautiful

Son

Be still while you stare into the sun

That burning and crackling hum?

That's the sound of your carnal cataracts burning and
breaking down some

Soon you will permanently see the moon

Even in the brightest of day

Most cannot see what is right in front of their face

Take a moment

Take two

Ride the wind

Let it carry you

No, no not your physical prison of a body

But rather your spirit

Your soul, your being and mind

Because after all, that's all you can take when you leave
your body behind

Don't seek control

Don't desire to capture but rather captivate and hold

For an effervescent moment

And that memory that no one else will remember will be all
yours

You will own it

But that too is but a whisper in the wind

Son

Be still as you stare into the sun

Writer's block

Who or what is the aid of your writer's blockade

I know the feeling all too well of reaching into your own
soul

Empty handed

Down in the doldrums of the ever dry inkwell

The words fester under the skin until it swells

Chaos is my muse

I'm a user

She's my drug, but I don't mean to abuse her

Haven't lost my life

But I've lost my love

I haven't lost my words

I'm drowning in them

Don't you dare try and pull me out

I like you

No, I really do

I like you like using a public restroom

I like you, like stepping in a mysterious puddle wearing socks

I like you like a hang nail

A cyst

I like you like all in one receiving every blow from a fist that ever missed

I like you like vinegar in my eyes

I like you like an IRS surprise

I like you like a sharp nagging pain in my lower back

I like you like conjunctivitis

Dermatitis

Hepatitis B

I like you like H.I.V

Is that too extreme?

Anyways

I like you like working all week for no check

I like you like a wool sweater with many tags itching my neck

I like you like other people's bad ass kids that have no fucking respect

I like you like a cheating lover

I like you like still damp but put down anyways sheets and
covers

I like you like being oppressed, unappreciated and stressed

I like you like living in a house infested with roaches,
bedbugs, rats, and silver fish

I like you like I'm starving and someone thought it was
funny to eat my only dish

I like you like overwhelming pungent body odor funk

I like you like finding a breast lump

I like you like Donald Trump

Hands up don't shoot!

I was minding my own business

Just trying to commute

I'm not talking back or trying to be cute

I was just wondering; what's the matter

What's the dispute?

I thought you were to protect and serve

No officer that's not drug money or loot

It's actually an honest week's wage

None of this makes sense, does not compute

My Hands are up don't shoot!

Don't taze or pepper-spray

If I'm not under arrest then I'll just be on my way

Wait! Don't sh......

It's like everything is just a memory

A distant, distant dream

Foggy standstill or so it seems

Detest what is evil and cling to what is good

I tell myself that but stay stuck in the hood

My circle has gotten so small it's a speck

Got my angels on my shoulders

But these demons breathing down my neck

Rodney Dangerfield status "I get no respect"

Got to focus! Not looking to the left or right, eyes fixed
forward in a determined stare

Because what lurks on the sides lines is tearing at my flesh
and yanking at my hair

They want to take me down and out

Curb stomp every positive thought from my mind and
mouth

Leave me in the gutter

To be washed away

No remnants left behind

But I'll stay my course

And try to stay sober while I walk this line

It's late…

So late, it's actually early

That time when the birds are clearing their throats to sing

And the sun isn't quite out of bed

It seems like every last crack, meth, or spike head has
crashed or settled down

The streets are empty

Not a person around

The distant sound of a car driving by

Every now and again

The sweet aroma of morning dew suspended in the air

The sun is beginning to rise and

You can feel its energizing warmth

But you're not aware

Standing under the willow tree

Watching comfortably

Aaaaaaaaaaand there's a spider in your hair!

You reading this!

Yes, You!

Its right there!

Oh wait….it was just a fuzzy

36

Sorry for the false alarm

Shit, that kind of threw everything off

clears throat cough, cough

Poems done

Piss off

There's this rash that itches so good

But if you scratch it enough it will bleed

But you keep scratching and scratching

And it kind of feels like satisfaction

Until it's stinging

And the blood is beading

Bright red gleaming

This isn't an analogy

We are candles

Burning ourselves out

To give other people our light

It's alright

Though the sorrow may last through the night

Joy comes in the morning

Warning!

Happiness is an effervescent thing

Not something to be clasped or grasped

But to rather be pursued

Because life is about the journey not the destination

Don't look too far into the future

Never mind the past

Right now is a gift

That's why it's called the present

I'm fine with being peasant

I may be poor in spirit

But I'm rich in soul

My bank account may be deficit

But my heart is full

Playing the hand I was dealt, trying not to fold

We're not born of a spirit of fear

Courage isn't an absence of fear or fright

It's a drive to persevere despite it

So take every ounce of doubt

Light a match

And ignite it

Had a taste of my own medicine

Got my stomach sick

But made me strong

Sure it was gross

Probably just got the dosage all wrong

I heard you are what you eat

If that is the case

I'm my own words

Which are for the most part verbs

I was left to my own devices

I reverted back to my vices

Hey! Look at me go....

Where are you going?

I don't know

Correction

Everywhere

Land and sea

Reaching for the air

~

Lying lurking snake in the grass

No code of ethics

No morals or scruples

No respect

Spineless coward

Insidious poltroon

Bumbling belligerent buffoon

No common courtesy

No common sense

Waste of human flesh

Yet you prosper…

~

It was a warm mid-summer evening

I finished my dinner and made my way outside to the front porch

My father had already polished off a twelve pack

Before I closed the living room door

He made sure

I was done

Son, you better have finished everything on that plate

I couldn't have been any older than eight

I smiled bright and let him know I surely did

Sat out on the front stairs

Looking into the sky

Marveling at the shifting clouds and wonderful array of sunset colors

And then with a crash and a bang

The door swung open

And in three to four long strides

My father was at my side

He lifted me up by my hair and launched me into the house

I learned how to land

But still got rug burns on both my elbows and hands

And then he proceeded to whoop my ass

My mom grabbed his arm in mid swing

What the fuck are you doing!?

Little lying bastard wants to waste his food

Not in my house!

I sat on the floor dazed and confused

While my mother explained that she wasn't feeling well
and he had mistaken her plate for my own

He sobered up pretty quick

The look of shame and disgrace washed over his face

With a thought bubble of "man I'm a dick"

My mother gave him the death stare

"Fix it!"

So we went outside and sat down as he apologized

For some reason this made me cry even more

He rubbed my head

It was still stinging and sore

He was at a loss for words

But stern and adamant he told me this

That whoopin is for the next time you mess up

I was wrong and I'm sorry

My tears subsided and my sadness turned into resentment

So what does that mean?

I asked

You get a "free pass"

I smiled and laughed

A free pass?

Next time I get in trouble; you won't kick my ass?

Watch your mouth!

But that doesn't count?

I had to double check

He could see the cogs turning in my little mind

But he had already done what he had done

He smiled, already knowing what I was thinking

Just make it count, and be sure to remind me, he said

I smiled back, my cheeks still rosy red

Eyes still lined with tears

With all types of malicious plotting formulating in my little mind

The next day

I got away

With knocking over his beer pulling his hair and slapping clean across the face

He jumped to his feet ready to give me the beating of a life time

Without reproach I told him

No, no remember my free pass

He sat back down and laughed

Okay but that's it

I smiled and handed him the towel I had ready

I sat down next to him

And he looked to me just like

I was looking to that sunset

He created a monster and he realized it

~

In this world

A man is either an anvil or a hammer

So I bring that click clack

Calamity clamor

And I'm not gonna hesitate

And it's never gonna jam up

So if you got beef

Don't be chicken

Ham up

I have hunger pains

And there is a banquet beneath your blouse

Below your waist

I haven't even begun, yet I can taste

That ever so sweet water on my tongue

You bite your lip

And without words

Your bedroom eyes beckon me

"I'm so wet"

"It's all yours"

"Come get it"

I love your sweet sector

Perfect little honey pot

Dripping nectar

Never thought I'd see a pussy so pretty

I almost want a picture of her for my wallet

So tight, so right, so fragrant

But not covered up with perfume

Your flower's natural pheromones in bloom

It drives me crazy, up your walls

This is no exhibition but rather an adventure

An exploration

Your body is the map

G marks the spot

And I care to attentively trace it with my lips, tongue, teeth,
and everything I got

Periodically I have to stop

Breathe, focus, focus, breathe

I let out a little laugh

I cannot believe

(Every sentence spoke is a concentrated stroke)

You're so fuckin hot!

You're about to climax and you look into my eyes

You ask

How much do you love me? Don't stop!

I go into overdrive

Oh I'm not!

Beyond words, a lot

Then you writhe and smile all sexy and wild

"Well"

"Love is sleeping in the wet spot"

Who do you think you are!?

Well, I suppose my name wouldn't quite suffice

I am 27 years of vice

All that I have endured so far yet

I'm the underdog in the bet

Who do I think I am?

Shit, I'm like…the man

Compared to most

I'm a compost heap stinking in the heat

In other words

I'm the shit

I'll smear ya lip

Dirty Sanchez, break ya hip

Lost

Wish it had been my wallet or a set of keys

I would have settled for less than this

But please oh please

I've lost my way

Once I was lost in your eyes

A couple of times

I've lost my mind

I'm losing my grip

It's either let go or hold on tight

And watch it all rip

A part of me has died

No funeral

No wake

I must man up for my own sake

But

I'm stuck in this rut

Sigh

So very much like Kill Switch Engaged

This is my curse

We may be in the same story but we are never on the same page

Never there when she needs me

Always there when she needs her space

It hurts my heart

It burns up my throat

What a bitter taste

Yet, I have hope

And I pray that may be an antidote

For the poison that is so very much a part of me

I would cut it all out

If I knew it wouldn't bleed me out

It seems like the majority now

Once upon a time when all was well

She thought of me as a Prince

Now

I make her wince

And another man holds her heart and hand

"May I have this dance?"

I can hear him say

And it's like another layer of me fades away

Into the deepest of black and what returns replaces what I lack

But it's icy and cold

It's not right, but I don't fight

Don't want to succumb to the numb

How did I become the bad guy?

All I really wanted was love

But I always hurt the ones I care for the most

I always lose them

I'm always lost

How can I pay the price, when I don't know how much it cost?

Would my life do?

If she could smile again

How much would it be worth?

Probably a few measly pesos or yin

Not even enough to buy a watered down shot of gin

To ease the pain

Maybe every now and then…she would think of me and
smile

It's more realistic to think she would cry

But these are my thoughts and I will imagine the best I can

That once upon a time, all was well and we never had a sad
story to tell

That I never fell from her good graces

And as she runs through my mind and my heart races to
keep up

I pace myself and ponder

What is it she chases?

Or is she just running away…away…away?

Take

Take a breath

Take a step back

Take a good hard look

Take that!

Take a break

Oh, no…no I don't mean some brief repose

Take this left jab

This right hook to your nose

Take a moment and let it sink in

For God's sake!

I meant heart break!

How does it feel?

You can't even imagine because you're not even real

Take all you have left and push it to the right

Take your licks!

Man up!

Fight!

No…no take it like a bitch

Put your fucking hands down!

Take that tone out of your voice

And that glare from your eyes

Take your own medicine!

Take what you have done to my life

Take all the pain I have endured and make it yours

I'll let you know when we are even

I'm taking all my stuff

I'm leaving…

Take me back

Take me for what I am

Take me for granted

Take me away

If there is one promise I know you will never break

It's that you will take and take and take

A letter to my fetter

How can it be that when I look at you and you look to me,
my heart no longer bleeds? It swells, it flares around the
seams, and it tears. I've only written this in my mind a
hundred times. Now I grow weary of the wordplay and the
rhyme, so I'll spill it out free verse.

I love you but I hate you. I wish you well and I truly want
the best for you, but that is not me and I no longer wish to
be in this relationship. I never saw this coming, but really
the blind don't see very much and now I have re-acquired
the knack of not feeling, but it's inconsistent like most
things in this life.

It's strange and when I say strange I mean fucked up and
sad that in this relationship the one thing that was most
consistent that we had was me letting you down and
breaking your heart. I hope that we can both learn from
this and take away something positive rather than
subtracting some load bearing column from our temples.
But if you must be ring around the rosies pockets full of
posies and we all fall to ashes, hopefully we can start a new
and rebuild.

I feel burdened. My heart has never been this heavy, like a
tungsten fist lurking in the shadows behind my ribs. How
does one sucker punch themselves like this? It's absurd,
it's ridiculous, tragic, lame, and a multitude of other words
that escape me. You mentally and emotionally raped me.
No cold shower here. A little uneasiness but I wouldn't

call it fear. I will be just fine, not really. Today I was envious of a co-worker who has colon cancer...I mean really! What the fuck!? How sick, sad, and depraved am I? I can barely look myself in the eyes, and when I do all I see is hate, hurt, pain, and my inner child naked running through the ice cold rain with nowhere to go.

I'm a case of basket case, a hot mess, maybe cold slop. But...I...can't...stop. I want you to not care about me but give credit where it is due, and if you feel like there is none deserved in my direction, well fuck you! Hope you have a happy life. Stay away from the drugs and the knife. Don't beat yourself up and watch out for creeping ego. Learn to humble yourself and shut the fuck up. That's all I have for now...yupp.

Cruzcampo and a good ole time

Rota, Seville, Cadiz, and Juarez Spain

Drink until I'm blind to keep the thought of you far away from my brain

My cerebellum burns almost as bad as my heart

Tear apart this paper like pericardium is mission status

I'll rip the ventricles apart...

Yeah that's where I'll start

Drink and smoke to make up for lost time

Deep...deep we dove below the cold dark ocean

Where you are a slave to the same ole days and its constant rocking motion

Eager we did await

Just to be on land

Just to be away from the monotony of the mundane

We were embattled

Me, myself and I

But in the end we made amends

And bought countless rounds

Cruzcampo you calm the beast

Cruzcampo you don't soothe my soul but you make me forget it at least

Cruzcampo you are only a few pounds...or euros

Whatever this monopoly money may be

Cruzcampo you stifle the misery

Dusk has set and I must retire before dawn

But before I do so I'll pack my sack with a few more
bottles and cans

But we have to keep it hush hush and kept away from the
Man

Till tomorrow Cruzcampo

Then I'll see you again

A series of haikus

Haiku, how are you?

Life is a catch twenty-two

That sure is the truth

Man of deep waters

Content in his discontent

Drowning in himself

Blanketed in warmth

So comfortable, just right

But work will not wait

Petrichor pungence

It literally just rained

I'm soaked to the soul

Rain, rain go away

Sunshine, grace me with your warmth

Too hot, come back rain

Life is a lesson

Appreciate the small things

They are what matters

Be careful not to,

Beard the lion in his den

There resides his kin

Cherish what you have

Before you no longer can

Life is but a breath

Learn from your mistakes

But learn from others as well

For life is too short

Take it serious

Life is funny, but no joke

Just ask the sad clown

Wait, I thought haikus

Were supposed to be about…

Nature? Whatever!

Don't sweat the petty

And don't you pet the sweaty

Go wash your damn hands

Do me a favor

Hygiene is quite important

Wash your frickin ass!

     Okay that is it

     Sorry, haikus are all done

     Fine! Maybe just one

          Oh shit, your still here

          Well, this is rather awkward

          Go away now, bye!

sigh seriously?

Just turn the page already

You are persistent

     Just the other day

     I came down from my high

     Had a sinking feeling in my soul

     And I realized what I have done

     And have failed to do

Thought to myself

"What's the best thing going on in my life?"

And I could only think of you

Then in my mouth

I threw up

Almost bust a seam

Belly laughing

So hard it felt like I got struck in the gut

Almost forgot

You're a nasty skanky brutal bottom feeding trash bag slut

New York, New York

The city so nice they named it twice

You are beautifully grotesque

Full of inspiration and full of vice

I missed you so

Don't want to leave

But somewhat glad to go

Just a road slash business trip with my bro

Don't get it twisted

You'll always be a peace of my heart

Your tarnished metal clothed in street art

Graffiti tags, bricks with patina

Sexy, sophisticated lean demeanor

Vodka from a crystal skull

Red bull

Hindu Kush on deck

Let's set it off

Re-flash watch is set

I'm lit, it ain't shit

It is what it is kid

He without sin cast the first stone

Well, anybody?

No?

Guess were all alone

I find it funny yet so lame

You point out the spec in my eyes

While yours burn bright with a wilderness in flames

Make your accusations and inconsequential claims

They are worth their weight in garbage

You harbor resentment in your heart and mind

All the while you preach forgiveness and peace

You are a conundrum to say the least

You do as I have done but say it is not the same

Do me a favor and do away with the nonsense and childish games

Live

Never survive

You only got one life to give

We all die but we don't all truly live

More people fail to try than fail trying…shit

We all have God given talents

What's yours?

Dig deep, take a jump, and leap

Don't treat them like a set of chores

You're unique

Fuck what haters say

Those who are too afraid to follow their own dreams

Will always try to discourage yours

Life is a party, don't surround yourself with bores

To survive is to scrape on by

Despite your hardships

Endure

What doesn't kill you will only make you stronger

Many of us been through hell and back

For some it takes us longer

Don't focus on what you lack

Negativity breeds negativity, fact!

Count your blessings

No worries

No stressing

When push comes to shove get to pressing

Get on your knowledge and learn

Life is a lesson

Insanity is doing the same thing over and over

Expecting different results

Step outside of yourself

Fix the problem without fixing the blame

Who cares whose it is!

Stop being a lame!

Your wasting time

Get on your grind

To live is so much more than to simply exist

Rolling with the punches and throwing your own fists

It's finding a way to rejuvenate the old

Taking garbage and turning it into gold

And when you're down

Find the upside, it's there

Lock your eyes, focus, and stare

Put in work and make moves

Don't be concerned with fitting in

Stand out and groove

Keep hope alive

Live never survive

I live with two familiar strangers

I can see the danger in that

The only catch is it's my wife and I

She felt defiled, ran off and had some other guys child

And now my heart is Where the Wild Things Are

I no longer recognize the man in the mirror

I walk away and forget

This heart break is legit

Nothing bent

Time wasted?

Time spent

What do I do?

I haven't the slightest clue

Took a long stroll down the socio path

After the aftermath

Took a shower, no time for a blood bath

Sigh

Gone with the wind

If only I could be chaff

You are my sunshine

My only sunshine

You make me happy, when skies are black

You'll never know dear

How much I love you

Please don't take my sunshine back

Because the sky would open and swallow itself

You may be my better half but without you I'm a detriment
to my health

A sickly sad ticking time bomb with nothing to lose

This love is no joke

Like a heart attack followed by a stroke

Serious

I'm at the end of my rope

Dangling as I choke

So cut this noose with the same knife I embedded in your
heart

This could be the beginning of the end

Shall we start?

Thoughtless I left you restless

Blatant disregard turned you reckless

Now I have nothing left but this rope necklace

One more step and this will be the last time you ever leave
me breathless

I just want to ramble for a second.

Strictly opinion and perspective (backed up with fact and common sense)

People: not everyone but a great and vast majority of people have no respect, love, morals, common courtesy, empathy, loyalty, shame…I can go on and on and I'm sure you can as well.

You reading this may be that type and not even know it!

For the most part…it's not your fault. A person is viewed as "for the most part" a conglomerate of what they have encountered and have endured throughout their life. Where you are from, how you were raised, religion, culture, yadda yadda yadda.

You are your decisions. You are the decisions you make, but oh brothers and sisters, you are certainly the decisions you refuse to make, walk away from, ignore, or think about for sooo long it's just "too late"

You are how you respond, how you adapt, how you roll with the punches. But remember this as well, although your past decisions and mistakes and heinous "we don't talk abouts" are a part of you

THEY DON'T DEFINE YOU!

People are generally good. People can change for the better just as they can change for the worse.

We have to pay it forward, we have to devise a plan!

What is wrong with this?

Why and how is it wrong?

How do we fix it?

What can we do to fix it? How soon?

What or who stands in our way? Why?

How do we overcome said obstacles?

We have to educate ourselves and our children!

Before you say some slant shit out the side of your neck like "PPPSSSSHHH I is educated! I'm Woke"

Being uneducated is not a laughing matter. Even though it has grown to be a custom of ours to laugh at the foolish, stupid, clumsy, and downright unfortunate. Being educated and knowledgeable just helps everyone. It certainly helps yourself! I have met plenty of stupid smart people. Think about it. We all have one or two of those people.

Brilliant, genius, mathematician type but socially inept, no common sense awkward and then you have the dim wit but highly attractive ever so shallow bitch or douche bag. I know. I know! There are plenty of other types and in betweens but you get my drift. People are people. Plain and simple. It astounds me. The holy preacher is capable of a heinous atrocity and the monster an act of compassion.

I am white hot incandescent rage in boots

A class delta fire submersed in the ocean that is me

My conscience tells me my angels and demons are in cahoots

My hearing is acute

My listening selective

Attention to detail is my elective

My major is self-aggrandizing glory

My minor is English

I've been writing this same fucking paragraph

To this same fucking story for years

Pardon my French

But this was supposed to be a synch

When push comes to shove, I didn't move an inch

Hold your applause please

I gave myself enough rope to be properly lynched

And crumbled to my knees

I suppose I should pray

Does anyone find it amusing that my muse use to abuse me?

I do to a degree

It's a dog eat dog world and ever since that bitch bore me

People act as if they adore me, but really I don't know why

Is it because even when I'm flat on my back I strive to be a standup guy?

Sure, its enthralling; falling from a high place

Until the impact pushes your face to the back of your head

Guess I'll quit my bickering

Could be worse

I could be physically dead

Don't play coy

All fur coat no trousers

Bass ackwards boy

No one wants to hear your heavy laden air

Don't complain about how it's unfair

You sent your inner child to foster care

You have no one to blame but yourself

We have tried to help time and time again

But you have proven that you are an insidious detriment

To yours and everyone else's emotional health and well being

This isn't just walking away

Its fleeing

It was a beautiful spring day

Laying in the green, green grass

On the other side

I decided to rest beside

A tall and firmly grounded maple

Basking in the shade it cast

My life began to fade into some sort of fable

Through my sun spotted peripherals

I witnessed a murder

Of crows

One of them flew from its flock

And landed not too far from my feet

I peered over my toes

I said hello and expected to the old crow

To bellow, caw, or croak

But much to my surprise

It spoke

"Some sleep walkers claim to be woke"

"I have heard some of the blind chime that they have
opened their third eye"

"Busy is an anagram for buried under Satan's yoke"

"Life is funny, if you're in on the joke"

So I asked

What does this all mean?

He sighed before he replied

The sunshine glistening from its ebony wings

"It's not because a bird is happy that it sings"

It ruffled it feathers

"If I have to explain then you weren't actually listening"

That's the way the cookie crumbles

The world mumbles

Under it's breathe

Not enough moxy or energy left

To speak out loud, bold, and proud

"It cowers beneath our grasp"

Together they laughed

"We can do great things"

The boy sings

"If we get our asses in gear"

"Do you hear?"

He asked

She smiled and laughed

"I'm one step ahead"

She said

The boy blushed, turning beat red

They embraced, looking deep into her eyes he licked her face

Then the boy turned and put two in the worlds head

Chocolate chips and lead

"That's the way the cookie crumbles"

And the world bled

I long to rest

Pressed up against billowing breasts

The comfort there is beyond compare

The sweet and spicy scent of your natural musk

This is my solace

Your heart beat and my own

When we are in one another's saccharine embrace

I can feel your aura permeating my skin

Down into the bone

I've never known

Such a comforting place

Think I'll call it

Home

Once upon a moment

I prayed for brokenness

Oh, He answers prayer

It's all very humbling

I've began crumbling

And have never known such despair

It's almost as if I am collapsing into myself

But my Lord is no liar

And He said He will never give me more than I can bare

So I thankfully walk into the refiner's fire

Knowing He is faithful to complete the work he has started
in me

Until that day

I wait, patiently

Double minded

Two faced hypocrite and cur

Won't you take a long hard look in the mirror?

Your cognitive dissonance is utterly absurd

Maladaptive reasoning and delusions of grandeur

You're a wolf in sheep's apparel

Oh sure, it's so couture

But it will never obscure your primitive and feral ways

Your word is worthless, why do you abscond so quick?

We both know all too well a dog returns to its vomit

So steer clear from my heard

For this shepherd doesn't brandish a rod or staff

But rather a twelve gauge Mossberg

The blind are no longer leading the blind

They kind of just mill around most of the time

Spouting out their emotions without properly thinking

I broke it down for you

But you just stand there in a daze blinking

Just because you have thoughts

Doesn't necessarily mean you are thinking

The population of dreamers, and genuine brave people that
can think for themselves seems to be dwindling

Surely shrinking

Go back to your television

And pissing the night away drinking

Without a care or worry in the world

Or get off your ass and be the change you seek

That ray of hope may seem bleak

But oh...wait!

Never mind a new nude photo of a celebrity was just
leaked

What happened to my people?

Shits weak!

My friend adversity

I spit in the face of adversity, not knowing: he was a friend

He didn't flinch, flee, break, or even bend

He sent his best regards and proceeded to contend

He didn't recede despite my anguished pleas

He just winked and grinned

Kicked me in the stomach and slugged me on the chin

My very breathe left me as I buckled to my knees

Then, lending me a hand, he spoke

"Fools hate discipline, on your feet my good man"

"How much of you will you ever know, if you won't work
through the pain it takes to grow?"

I smiled in the face of adversity with bloodied gums

He smiled back

"Your countenance has changed"

I shrugged, opened my arms wide for a hug, but yet again
he attacked

In a hurried fury of elbows, knees, feet and fists

But every blow he did throw

Missed

I leaned in and gave him a kiss and a pat on the back

Ah, adversity you are a blessing

I've learned my lesson

You'll have to try harder than that

Mask Maker

Mask maker, mask maker

Make me a mask

One that will properly cover up all the past

The wrinkles and laugh lines

Nostalgic markings that have been left behind

This face is but a memory

You have never seen your own face

Only pictures and reflections

In this insurrection I no longer recognize myself

Mask maker, mask maker

Cover up this handsome obscenity

Mask maker mask maker give me a new identity

Remember?

Remember when a bag of chips was 25 cents?

Remember when it was common for people to have common sense?

Remember that thing we said we would never speak of?

I ain't sayin shit relax!

Remember when the Italians had everything on lock?

Remember when your kids could play down the block?

Remember when fools would hide their money in their sock?

Remember when people had manners and respect?

Well sorry Miss Aretha

We replaced that with heroin, meth, and eatha

And the dealer is fifteen with a glock and he don't care either

Remember when people had shame?

Well shit, some things change and some never will

Hitler's youth patrolling the streets all about that almighty dollar bill

Without any form of honor they'll kill

Some misunderstood kid doing a bid

Be out in fifteen years and do it again

Remember the knockout game?

This white guy told me it was a myth

Only I seen that shit with my own eyes...he don't get the drift

It wasn't called the knockout game

It was called just cuz or fuck that lame

Take his shoes and take his chain tell him to never come round the block again

Remember when a working class hero was something to be

And we weren't all too consumed by the media, shit hasn't been right ever since

Remember when we would make like rise against

And swing life away

I remember everything like an elephant listening to five finger death punch

I remember when I whooped your ass for trying to take the money for my lunch

I remember giving you my last dollar to my name and

The shirt off my back and down the road you shit on my name

I remember when we were tight

I remember ruining that over a girl

Who was, is, and continues to ruin my life

Remember that fight?

Remember five gallons of wine in between the three of us?

Remember when the Centro bus didn't have cameras?

Remember when we were so young it use to be "what if?"

Now it's remember that an remember this

Remember when I would shut the hell up and pass the spliff?

Remember me? Remember B? Well I'm back like you didn't put postage on it

I'm here for the world and I'm posted on it

If you do anything remember who you are and where you're from

Give back and get some

I ducked and dodged

Yet I still have these scissors lodged in my heart

I'd pull them out if I knew it wouldn't tear me apart

Buddhists say life is suffering

Well maybe I can turn my suffering into art

Beware, I am a bungee pit

With a first aid kit

Enough sustenance for you to survive

A wonderful view

Shifting patch of blue

But no Wi-Fi

Out to sea

Angles & Dangles

List & Trim

30 foot waves come crashing in

Don't wince at the avulsion of skin, limb, or next of kin

Pray we have no loss of propulsion

Stow for sea

Don't you dare make a sound!

Rig for reduced electrical

We ran a ground

Code red

Finally, on our way home

It's all a dream, purgatory the cook says

Were already dead

Prodigious prejudice

You think I should register this Four-Five?

This AK, this AR, this Glock, this Nine?

Who are you to tell me how to live my life?

Fuck this, it's pointless

Now you're at the end of my knife

Anoint this

Appoint this

White boy to power

Immediately, expedite that shit within the hour

You're bitter?

Well I have a taste for that sour

I will ravage and devour

I stand tall while you cowards cower

Topple you like a poorly built tower

Call you Eiffel

Butt you with the end of your own rifle

Hold your mouth and nose closed

Suffocate and stifle

I'm your asthma attack

Leave your lungs ruptured and your sternum cracked

You'll die shortly after that

Reader! You are far more than you know. You are far more than your mistakes or perceived to be shortcomings or flaws. You are beautiful. You are fearfully and wonderfully made. There is a system constructed that is meant to render you powerless. You are not powerless. You are a spirit in a human condition. A radiant glowing ball of incandescent light. You are loved, deeply, madly, truly. Don't give up. Don't you dare give up! Every hardship is a test. I know there are a lot of trials and tribulations. You are not alone in this. You are not alone in this. What you have done and what you have not doesn't matter. Don't allow regret or worry to drag you down. Dream on! But wake up.

You can change the world, but first you have to change yourself. Let the negativity wash away. You are a blank canvas. People are products of their environments, yes. People are a collection of experiences, memories, fears, thoughts, beliefs, baggage, hopes, dreams, aspirations, ideas and so much more. But we decide, it is our choice what to hold on to and what to let go of. You are more than your current issues and circumstances. You are More than your current issues and circumstances!

You are seed of a beautiful tree, breaking through its shell, growing, stretching reaching for bigger, brighter, and better things.

You are limitless. Don't listen to the negativity of others. Those who are too afraid to follow their own dreams will always try to discourage yours. You are not born of a spirit of fear. Its spoon fed to you from birth. Purge yourself of it. Meditate on the good. Come into your being. You are strong! You are mighty! You are different if you only choose to be. You can. You can! You will. I believe in you.

Let go of all your pain. Let go of all your worries. Expel it from you, close your eyes and take a deep breathe in until you can't anymore. Hold it. Slowly but forcefully exhaling imagine darkness and doubt and fear, anger and pain leaving you like a black mist.

Just like we bathe, we have to wash our hearts, our minds, and our inner selves. Purge it from your beautiful being. Don't let it back in.

Failure is not failure when you learn from it, move on continue, never give up!

I love you. Reader, I love you.

I'm on the edge of the ledge of life

I'm on the sharp end of that cold, cold knife

Can somebody, someone, successfully survive saving me?

She said, as her fragile flesh bled

It's such a rush

Anything to hush

The suppressed sorrowful silent cry

The pressure is just too much

So with precision

A little incision

All the pain and anguish

Momentarily subside

It's my decision

And plus

It's easy to hide

I

Do

It

On my

Thighs

(Sigh)

Life never turns out how we expect

So I hope for the best and expect the worse

And in doing this hope I can lift the curse

Of my damned heart break

It's beyond bent

It's like a hoarder's apartment

Holding onto broken promises and memories that will
never be of use

I come up with every excuse in the book

My shattered little keep sakes

I keep for a nostalgic look

Reminiscing of the good ole days that will never return

My options are spring cleaning

Or light a match

And let it all burn

There is some sort of deep seeded resentment in this
twisted malicious heart of mine

I find when I'm flustered it flares

Bursting at the seams here and there it tears

This is a love and hate relation ship that has set sail on
unprevailing winds

All that quickly rises will expeditiously descend

Whether or not it crashes and burns is on your end

I meant well

Yet the road to hell is paved with good intentions

I won't stand high on tall tales

Nor will I deny the truth

At much I did fail and I am an uncouth, adulterous,
insidious John Wilkes Booth

A visceral vessel of fleeting youth

I've done some thinking and I some ways you're like
Abraham Lincoln

For you stood for my emancipation

And I shot you down

You fell for nothing but me

Some may say

You fell for a nothing

But they don't know shit about me

You fell and we can tell you fell hard

I wasn't there to catch you at all

I far more than "dropped the ball"

Apologies are now hollow and hold no weight

And even if they did

It's far too late

You have revealed that you no longer feel the way you
once did

I can't hold that against you and I won't bother to try

What doesn't kill you will only make you stronger

And you damn near died multiple times

I've been told that I am a man of deep waters

But rather feel like a superficial shallow pond

These words aren't for me to abscond our violated sacred
bond

On the contrary, they are intended to set you free

From the prison that is me

For as long as we remain

You will always be some way fettered and chained

Ever so reminiscent of past torment and pain

I wish not to be a thorn in your side

In your heart I much rather reside

But you see, a parasite cannot deny its nature

You should take some time to listen to a song titled
"coward" by black light burns

I think that you have learned some time ago that this is me
to the T

You have given me the benefit of the doubt abundantly but
I have failed to receive

Though I do not wish to sell myself short

I have come a long way

But that does not subtract from the fact that I will only
break your heart again

That is a promise that I don't want to keep but is utterly
certain

Real eyes realize real lies

So I know you can see my words and how their steeped in
sincerity

You have always been able to see right through me with
such vivid clarity

But you're blind if you turn away from all the signs

Don't allow me to be your basket

When it's been your time to shine

Masses were massacred at the masquerade

There was a raid

Men in black masks with fully automatics and grenades

Rendered damn near unconscious I just laid

In the mass grave

Torn bodies, intestines and blood sprayed across my face

I'll never forget that metallic taste

My ears ringing

But I could still hear the singing

Of bullets and shrapnel ricocheting

I couldn't understand what the guy next to me was saying

He was muttering and blood was sputtering

All the time the music still played

Like some sick symphonic sanguinary game of charades

My eyes were stinging like I just been maced

I went to move

But my legs

My legs were no longer attached to my waist

Mother Mary full of grace

This mutilated middle aged woman began to pray

Then there was a bright flash and I awoke

Breathing heavily trembling cold and wet

I noticed my sheets were soaked

I was still in bed

I wiggle my toes

No broken bones

Nothing was open nor exposed

The stench of charred flesh still stunk up my nose

You were still sleeping deep

I got up quietly trying not to make a peep

Time to start the day

First I'll get some cereal to eat

Underway

Pack your bags

Or

Leave it all behind

Try and push all of it out of your mind

Shut up and do what you are told!

You may want to bring a jacket

This time a year

Hell gets pretty cold

I went to write

But my thoughts were asleep for the night

They hung a sign

"Come back tomorrow once you are occupied"

I let out a combination of a laugh and a sigh

WAKE THE FUCK UP!

I replied

They turned over ever so slight

Pulling the covers tight

I turned on the light and jumped up and down on the bed

Yet they were not roused

Suppose I'll get back to work instead

For now

If home is where the heart is, are the homeless heartless?

If you're broken hearted, do you automatically reside in a broken home?

If you wear your heart on your sleeve do you fold it up like a pack of cigarettes in the 50's?

Could unrequited love be considered heart disease?

Have you ever experienced heart break?

Heart ache?

Is a heavy heart always hardened?

I'd like to know

I heard that God helps those who help themselves

Have you heard that?

Everything is relative, so to a degree it has some truth

I personally like to help the downtrodden

The homeless vagabond

The misguided youth

Maybe I can help you

I heard that if you give a mouse a cookie

He'll want a glass of milk

I also heard that if you give "them" a foot they'll want a
yard

I don't think that is about the mouse

But I would share my house and my yard

And I'll walk with you

But I rather keep my shoes and certainly my feet

I heard that it is better to have loved and lost than to never
have loved at all

That must be true

Because I didn't hear it at all

Actually I read it in a bathroom stall

Similes make me smile

Unless you are comparing me to the likes of him

Or them

If you have a pair of paradoxes would you have quadradox?

Has anyone ever found out what happens to all of our socks?

Can chickens get chicken pox?

Are you wondering what you are reading?

Maybe you can do better

Remember this

Its poetry, writings, and ramblings

Remember this

Write your old friend a letter

And don't leave the house without giving your lover another kiss

Ignorance is bliss

But it doesn't stand up in court

Common sense hasn't been common since......

Exactly

Oh and I will leave you with this

Don't take yourself so seriously, learn to laugh more and in everything

Strive

You won't get out of life alive

In retrospect

My favorite place was nuzzling the nape of your neck

Wrapped up

Intertwined

Producing body heat like an apartment with no air
conditioning in a Texas summertime

It wasn't about the sex

You helped heal my heart and mind

But the sex was amazing

Sucks I had to leave you behind

Never wanted to hurt your heart

Or leave you so alone

But hey

Neither of us will grow if we're not out of our comfort zone

If you choose to hate me

I understand and that's fine

But remember me in the winter time

God bless you

Evil eschew

Gesundheit

Salud

Righteousness is a virtue we all should aspire to

Burning bright reddish orange embers

Falling like snow in December

Carried by the wind

Brush fire conflagration

An arsonist's wet dream

Watch it pop crackle and gleam

Let us burn this bridge to ash

But do so as a team

I remember a time when I knew beyond the shadow of a
doubt that I could not go on living

That the pain was so immense

So thick, sticky, and dense

Depression like a pit of muck and mire

It sapped my strength to the point I was running on fumes

It snuffed the flickering flame of hope and desire

Cut the wick

Sick and tired of being tired and sick

Like fatigue and apathy were apparitions

Physical manifestations of all the stress and strife

Of what I had perceived at that time as a

"Pointless life"

In the matter of a year

I lost my mind, career, best friend and wife

I had my hands full

A handle of Jack Daniels

A noose, a gun, and a knife

But it was made aware to me

That suicide doesn't end the pain it just passes it on to
someone else

The thought of passing on my anguish to the ones I love

Helped pull me from the pit

There was a time when I knew beyond the shadow of a
doubt I couldn't go on living

I've never been happier to have been wrong

I have lived a good life

Despite the hardships, trials, and tribulations

I have learned from them

I have learned that every breakdown leads to a
breakthrough

Life will always put a great weight on your shoulders

Pace yourself and don't lock your knees

Perseverance builds character

Try your best to not grumble and mumble under your
breathe

Reality is your perspective

Your thoughts create your reality

So guard your heart and mind like a priceless treasure

Negativity breeds negativity like a cesspool

We are but vessels

We must be cleansed

Meditate on the good, right, and wholesome of the world

When you are full to the brim of pain, anger, and
frustration

Spill it out onto paper

Get it out of you

Artistic self-expression is a sweet remedy to all that ails
you

Let go of the ego

This one time

This one time I witnessed lightning strike the ocean

To be specific it was the Pacific

I was deployed on my third and final fast attack Submarine

I have witnessed many things

But this may just be the most beauteous and serene
occurrence I have ever seen

It was a brightly star lit night

There wasn't a spec of land in sight

We had been under for weeks

My watch just ended and although I was exhausted I
figured I would get some fresh air

And smoke a cigarette or three

Once I was topside in the tight quarters of the sail

The fresh ocean breeze caressed me, slightly calming my nerves

Then there was a low rumbling grumble of thunder

But there wasn't a cloud in the sky

Just starlight spread across far and wide

Her dark blue surface was placid when she was struck

The incandescent lightning spread asunder

Dancing across and throughout the crisp cold water

In that very moment it began to rain

I'll never forget it because it actually washed away some of my pain

I know that sounds cliché

But it's real

I'm trying my best to express something inexplicable to me and how it made me feel

For me, that day will go down in infamy

As a cherished keepsake that I will never forget

When I close my eyes and think, I can still see it

When I fell from her grace

I landed into between a rock and a hard place

Eventually I rose to my feet

Took a long look in the mirror

But the person staring back wasn't me

I couldn't look myself in the face

I felt emasculated, defiled, shamed, and disgraced

I heard them say time heals all wounds

But they never mention all the scars

Many moons have passed

And I have learned to love me for me

My perfect imperfections and little idiosyncrasies

Now I can look back and laugh

Wholeheartedly

I pray you will do the same

Blackberry Brandy

Blacker the berry, sweeter the juice

I knew this girl named Blackberry Brandy

And she was proud of her roots

Sweet but strong

Like you didn't bless the bottle

And swigged it all wrong

She brought out the best and worst in me

She was both a blessing and curse to me

Never had I known such pleasure

Never had I known such pain

She was educated and well spoken

But full of disdain

But oh! Those lips

Those eyes

Them hips

Them thighs

She healed my soul but left my heart broken

I've healed since then, all better now

But it took quite some time to put that

Blackberry Brandy down

I'm no hero

And you're no damsel in distress

I'm no hero

But I'll be much obliged to save you from this mess

I'm no zero

One, two, three

But for you baby I'll be what you want me to be

But I gotta warn you, I have some villainous tendencies

I'm no superman

Lay your restless head on this S-less chest

I'm no hero, and you're no damsel in distress

I can't leap buildings in a single bound

I can catch bullets but I'll be dead on the ground

I'm no hero but give me a chance

I'll even wear my underwear outside of my pants

Oh, blank paper

Dim lit computer screen

You are my sanctuary, you are my get away, my means to
an end

The vessel I pour my darkness in

You are my cleanse

I have learned to let it out and care not who it offends

I can only hope

That my readers can pick up this kaleidoscope

And peer through its lens

To see the pieces of them that are me

I talk to inanimate objects

Because I too know what it is like to be over looked and ignored

They never interrupt

Roll their eyes or convey that they are bored

Never are they preoccupied with their phone, pretending to listen

Simply waiting for their chance to speak

They never judge me or leak what I say when I confide in them

They are just there

And that is far more than I can say for people

Things my father told me as a child:

"I love you"

"Men don't cry, and crying and bickering solves nothing"

"Life, it's all a fucking joke and it's never going to be easy"

"If it's easy….it isn't worth it"

"It takes hard work, dedication, and resolve but above all else a positive attitude in order to be successful" "and that doesn't mean that you can't lose everything you worked for, for no reason"

"Shit happens" "Don't shit where you eat"

"If you want to know what your wife or girlfriend will look like in the future take a look at her mom"

"Don't marry an Italian or Spaniard"

"Stand your ground, even if you get beat into it"

"Don't give up ground, keep your hands up, don't lock your knees, and never back up, if anything side step"

"Don't pull your punches, imagine driving straight through your opponent"

"If someone is going to attack you in the streets, treat the situation as if they are trying to kill you"

"Don't start fights, finish them! But if you have the opportunity to walk away do it and you automatically win"

"Stay alert, Stay alive" "Paranoia is a state of alertness"

"Family first" "DTA, Don't trust anybody"

"Keep your head on a swivel, three hundred and sixty degrees"

"Don't be such a wise ass!"

"Whatever you do, do it well, put all of yourself into, even if its ditch digging, you dig the best damn ditches"

"Just don't get married"

"Pull my finger" "Get me another beer"

"You're grounded"

"I'll tell you when you are a man"

"Shut up and go to sleep"

These streets don't love you

They covet you

They thirst for your life

Blacktop, asphalt, cold cracked concrete strife

Beckoning you with venomous glossy lips

Hollow promises of stacks and bundles and bundles and stacks

Just gotta pull your weight in dirt

Put in work

Sell heroin and crack to misguided youth

Live by an eye for an eye and a tooth for a tooth

I know you're trying to provide

But can't you see it was designed to keep you institutionalized

The bible says what a man speaks is the overflow of his heart

Then why are you so quick to spit bars that tear your own people apart

Don't be deceived

They're not your friends

The goons, jackals, wolves, and hyenas

Gonna sing like canaries when they are subpoenaed

Get out while you still can

Put your foolish pride aside and be a better man

Set no limits, nothing is above you

Please listen, young man

These streets don't love you

What do I want?

I want justice

I want solidarity

I want all the lies and cover ups exposed

I want vivid clarity

I want an uprising, a revolution

We have identified the problem

Let's come up with a solution

Of course I would like the finer things in life

Financial freedom, acres of land, and a faithful wife

But some things just seem further out of reach than others

I have it pretty good compared to my brothers being
gunned down in the streets

His daughter was in the back seat

His name was Philando Castile, he had a permit to carry
and conceal

The police shot him in cold blood in front of his love

What the fuck is the deal!?

My heart is heavy, for real

How long will this senseless violence persist?

The media points their dirty fingers

We need to rise up as a tungsten fist

I fall in and out

Off and on

On a regular basis

I trip over

My own thoughts and words

More often than my untied laces

Head over heels

I tend to land on my myriad of faces

Trying to control, what's not in my control

I get so aggravated

Trying to not be so cold and frozen

Gotta let it go

And grab ahold of the kingdom

Because I believe I was chosen

Starving but not allowed to slaughter the cattle

That's one thing that grinds my gears and gives my cage a
rattle

That and listening to my so called peers prattle

Why is it that the people that don't have their lives together
are the one's trying to tell you how to live your life?

Meanwhile they are unarmored and blindfolded in battle
brandishing a butter knife

Life is funny

If you're in on the joke

Although the irony of it often forms like a lump in your
throat

If you can laugh at yourself

You can always be laughing with

Humor is the spice of life

And a marvelous gift

We got you where we want you. We haunt you. We watch you. We literally stalk you, but we make you agree, it's free to see you but you don't see "we"

We have slowed you down, made you fat, with fast food full of additives, preservatives and other chemicals you can't even pronounce

We have tainted your drinking water and the air you breathe

Fluoride calcifies your pineal gland but oh it's good for your teeth

We study you like rats in a maze

We control the media, your minds, and how you behave

We knew you wouldn't exercise or read if we provided thousands of channels for you to view

On your tell lie vision

We tell you when to sit and stand, we provide your great divide

We designed it to be that you practically have to break your back to get out of poverty

We have integrated technology into everything, making it oh so convenient and easy to use and abuse, that a child can do it, bet your kids already know how

Slowly over time, you have become dependent on your technology, we have fabricated your prison cell, and you actually want more bars

All we had to do is make a highly convenient tracking device, put games, and social media apps on it to keep you distracted

There are ways we can access your online bank accounts and even your home security systems

You tell us everything on Facebook, take pictures of it and post it on Instagram, all those funny filters on snapchat sure made it easy to build a facial recognition database

We have access to whatever we want, who among you reads the fine print before you consent?

That's what we thought

You have pretty filthy mind for someone so brainwashed

Whether you feel you mind is open or closed

There is surely still some blockage

So knowledge and common sense cannot properly flow

And to a degree you know

But you are conditioned by an administration you don't even know

Who, actually represent you and has absolute control

You just flip your hair and LOL

Very much obliged to sport their lies

Stuck under their yoke

Your gilded fetters and chains

You jingle jangle your bling blang as you choke

Either that…or you're broke

Living check by check

The vast majority of your existence is paying off debt

Student loans, mortgage, taxes, fees, fines, and tariffs

Only to be unarmed and gunned down by some incompetent Sheriff

Albert Einstein once said

"We cannot solve our problems with the same thinking we used when we created them"

Benjamin Franklin said "the definition of insanity is doing the same thing over and over again, expecting different results"

My flesh, bones, and brain call out for war

My heavy laden heart cries out

"No More"

Malcom X exclaimed

"Be peaceful, be courteous, obey the law, respect everyone; but if someone puts his hands on you, send him to the cemetery"

Now is not the time to be weary

Now is the time to be strong, steadfast, and firm

Now is the time for our brilliant minds to devise a plan

And exercise poise

And remember that same man once said

"Early in life I had learned that if you want something, you had better make some noise"

Round and round the cycle of perpetual debt goes

Never diminishing, it only grows

Your entire life is someone else's board game

You go to school

You get a job

Maybe go to college to get a better job

So you can pay off your student loans, mortgage, and credit card debt

The vast majority moving through life like an assembly line

Never thinking of ways to disrupt the cycle

Almost content in their discontent

Somethings got to give

This is no way to live

Will somebody someone save us from all this meaningless shit

I'm slowly concocting a plan

But I'm only one man

If you want to change the world, start with your self

That's the stage I'm at

But I'm calling out to you

Dear reader, let's impact the world

Let's throw a wrench in the cycle

I need you, we need you, and the world needs you

To be the change we seek

We meet every third Thursday of every week

Paper chaser

Paper chaser, paper chaser

Will you chase it to the grave?

You brag and boast of your meaningless escapades

You pride yourself on the fact that you don't know how to act

"Just get dat money"

Whether you have to steal, kill, sell your ass or hustle crack

Question for the cowards

How are you standing without a spine in your back?

Are you held together with all the knives your alleged homies now lack?

"Trap King"

"Trap Queen"

You're not royalty

You're ensnared and enslaved

That's not jewelry, I'm talking about your gilded fetters and chains

Fool's gold!

You would find a way to chase that paper if you lost your legs and became lame

"Money makes the world go round"

Is your mentality

All the while you grow deficit in your account of morality

It's quite unequivocal what your motive is

I could understand if it was on your heart to genuinely and generously give

Or contribute to good works and actually live

But it's not about love or education

Or even the future, which are actually the kids

It's about generating revenue

It doesn't matter to you who dies or who lives

Here's a little fun fact

Wealth is worthless in the time of wrath

You can't serve God and mammon

Let's see you put your money where your mouth is when the world is stricken with famine

This is the end of my rant and rave

But paper chaser, paper chaser

Will you chase it to the grave?

Broken hearted

Mending a broken home

Aspiring for perfection

This long road I roam

The problem with making your own path is

You can't hitch a ride

But I'm never alone

Me, myself and I

On the pursuit of happiness

Many atrocities I have seen

But there is a silver lining to everything

Oh how they gleam

How brave are the ones who progress?

Take life's beatings and stress, lift it up over their heads

Just to rest on their shoulders

A burden of unsurmountable boulders

You speak of drowning in your ashes as they smolder

The embers searing your lungs

If you believe we're getting older then that is your reality

But the phoenix does rise from its very own ashes

And as everything seems to break us down as it bashes, crashes and sometimes slashes us to ribbons

That pain is the true us breaking through the thought to be impregnable shell

There is beauty in the beast and a heaven to our own hell

And only time will tell

If we dare to stick around to listen to that liar

The ocean that crashes inside of our souls cannot extinguish the fire of our spirit

Are we on the edge of the ledge if life or just near it?

And when that deafening silence becomes too much to bare

Stop pulling at your hair

And listen

Because the answer was always there

Is it audacious to ask You to help me be Me?

I'm not what you think

I'm so much less

Yet more

I am a flowing stream

A gentle mist

A steady down pour

I am a frustration that gets you to the point where you just
collapse and laugh

Maddening

Deffening

Relapse

I'm your present

Future

Past

Is it too much to ask

for you to tell me who I am

I fully understand you are in an identity crisis of your own

I know its random but I can feel the darkness in my bones

Its contrary because you see me as a lamp

I shed light but I cast stones

Ask the man in the concentration camp why he feels so
alone

Far from perfection but we stay approaching

Just players in the game

We're only human, but animals all the same

Some a little more wild

Others a little more tame

Everyone bullshit posting

Stay coaching, but can't blow a whistle when they see the
poachers encroaching?

I won't run and I won't hide

Do my best to abide in the way of the Almighty God

Confident that I will survive whether or not I get shot

But I stay on the move

Never in just one spot

I too have an open heart and an open mind

We just have to make sure that we guard it most of the time

Roses are red

Violets are violet

GAT GAT GAT!!!!

12 gauge push your chest through your back

And all you ever knew

And everyone you ever loved will have to move on without you

Life is sudden, so is death, enjoy every breathe

Whether it's full of smoke and you cough and choke

Or it's deep and steady, heavy on your lover's neck

Black rose

While I was out, observing the streets

Strolling about, shuffling my feet

My eyes anxiously analyzing all around

They fell upon the cold, cracked concrete ground

To my utter amazement there grew a black rose

Someway, somehow, I suppose there must have been a
single seed with a distorted, deep rooted destiny.

Somewhat comparable to somebody I know

I still wondered how something so beautiful and brilliant
could grow out of something so hard and cold.

Perhaps it had some sort of contorted connection to the cold
alone

Even yet though, it was warm and compassionate, it did not
show.

But at last, that single seed, desperately determined to
succeed, grew and grew like a weed.

Over time, overturning, that cold, hard, cracked concrete

That black rose indeed anticipated its own flawless victory.

Ever watch something or someone grow into something so beautiful and know that your heart and your hands and your mind and time helped it grow?

And you would absolutely love

To feel that something, than someone

For real

But your hands now are like death

And you feel as if your slightest touch

Would be nothing but a detriment

And such thoughts and theories make you weary

At least you can observe from afar

Like drunken nights sitting on hills still wet from the rain

Drinking away your pain

And marveling at the stars

Currently in a great state of transition

My life has not come to an abrupt halt but rather a fork in
the road

And I have been assigned a new mission

Time to get out of the kitchen and clear my own path

Immerse myself in my aspirations and live to love and
laugh

I will try my best to not burn bridges

But I must confess I am a hot mess and an arsonist at heart

Nothing like a refiner's fire to redefine, reshape, and renew

I'm aspiring to be the change I seek

How about you?

You say life is a bitch and then you die

But...

You abused her and made her cry

What did you expect?

You met her crazy sister Karma

But still want to act like you don't know

You reap what you sow

What you neglect to prune and water won't only not grow

It will perish

She was designed for you to nourish and cherish

She longs to feed the humble and starving artist

But your selfish ways cut you off

From her bountiful harvest

I met the devil at church

He was charismatic and enthused

His beauty was bewildering

He smiled as if he was amused

But when it came time to sing praise

He adamantly refused

To live is to create

To grow, to build, to experience, to learn

To feel not just pleasure but pain

To appreciate the sunshine

To appreciate the rain

To endure, to persevere

To accomplish

To fall but get back up again

To triumph over any and every obstacle

Including yourself

To live is to shine your light as bright and for as long as
you can

Into the darkness

To fill the abysmal void with knowledge, memories,
wisdom, love, music, and art

Until they day we depart all the ones we love and have
impacted and shaped throughout our journey

To live is to change the world by first changing yourself

To live is to prosper and share the wealth you accrue

Life is about you

Investing in you

Anger is pain and frustration dressed up as power

But it's more

The lust for money is the root of all evil

That's why the banks fund our wars

A slant and depraved cycle of debt

To keep the people ignorant and poor

To divide by race, social status, and class

So they can control and conquer

The ninety-nine versus the one percent

The government isn't supposed to control the people

The people are supposed to control the government

I've been through a lot

So take this advice as you wish

Make a list

A bucket list if you will

Fill it with your wildest dreams

All your goals, make them big and outrageous

Don't put limitations on yourself, others will do that for
you

But pay them no mind

And if they don't support your dreams, I don't care who
they are

Give them none of your time

Don't work your life away at a job you hate surrounded by
people you don't like

Your life can end in the blink of an eye, so do as much as
you can now

Stop procrastinating

Travel the world, save your money, eat lunch with a
random stranger

Poor your love out into the world and don't do something
for someone just so they can do something in return

Laugh and learn often

Give thanks with a grateful heart

Get out and stay out of any sort of abusive relationship

Now!

You deserve better

Learn to love yourself for who you are before you settle down

Have integrity, that's doing the right thing even when no one is watching

Be courageous, courage is not the absence of fear it's pressing on despite it

Try new things, throw caution to the wind

Actually throw caution downwind so it doesn't come back and hit you in the face

Do what you love, what makes you come alive

Speak lovingly to yourself

Celebrate your accomplishments

Learn to control and analyze your own thoughts

Get rid of all negativity, including people, there is no place for it

Pay it forward

Stop making excuses

Dedicate ten thousand hours to a skill that you want to get better at

Spend quality time with the people you love, they won't be here forever

Never stop learning and educating yourself

And last but not least, understand this

You do not truly know yourself, you can be who and whatever you choose to be but you have to work hard at it and practically be obsessed with it, but don't put limitations on yourself and don't listen to all the hate and negative nonsense that the world will spew on you

Dust it off and keep going with the accomplished end result in mind

It will not be easy but I promise it will be worth it

Made in the USA
Lexington, KY
18 January 2017